For those parents who understand...
H.O.

This Book Belongs To:

_____

My unicorn is suspiciously wiggling,
She has a smile on her face!

She's starting to cross her legs,
To the toilet we race!

She's having trouble telling me,
When she needs to 'go'!
I ask her if she needs to potty,
And she always answers "no"!

Most unicorns don't use toilets,
But my unicorn is unique!
I want her to live inside with me,
So, she needs to learn this technique!

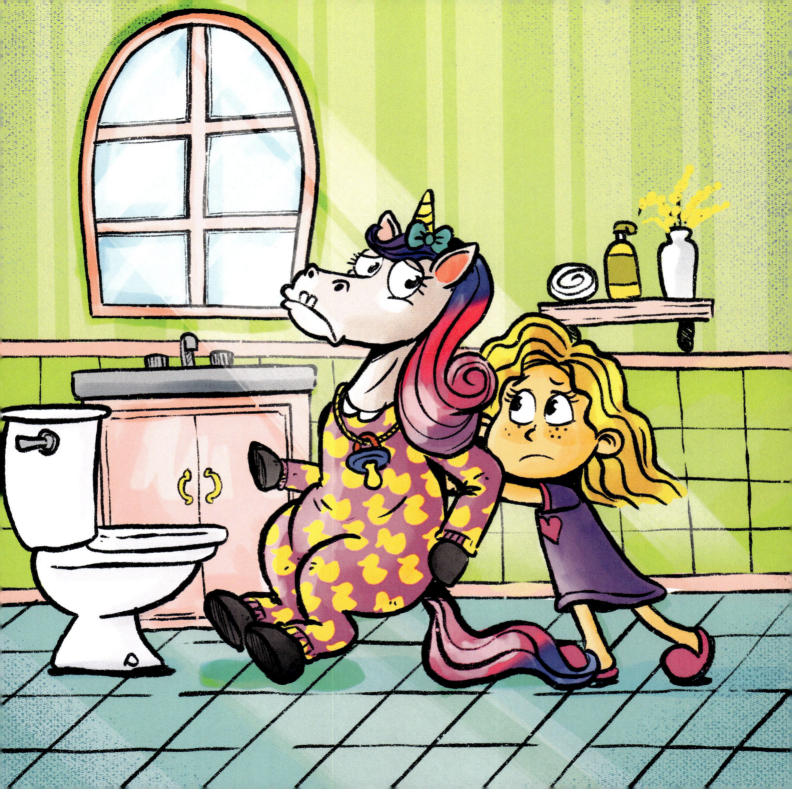

I buy her brand new undies,
That have a magical print!
Hoping she will take an interest,
She needs to get the hint!

I bribe her with toys and treats,
I've heard it's the way to go!
But she wants the reward without the work!
So I have to tell her "no"!

She's starting to think it's funny,
When she leaves a surprise on the floor!
She watches as I clean it up,
Laughing hysterical on all fours!

So I strip her down to nothing,
Leaving her no choice.

I'm scared to take her out of the house,
Because a toilet may not be near!
I am usually in a constant panic,
And in a regular state of fear!

I am trying to get clever,
To show my unicorn the way!
If she starts to keep her undies clean,
We can go more places and play!

Wait!

She's starting to seem more interested!
She is sniffing around the ground!

She'll stop if she catches me watching her,
So I'm trying to not make a sound!

She is getting so much bigger,
Look how much she's grown!

She has a BIG, PROUD smile,
She feels so CLEAN and DRY!
She is such a BIG GIRL now!
I'm so happy I could CRY!

WE DID IT!

I DID IT!

THIS CERTIFICATE IS AWARDED TO

_____

FOR BECOMING POTTY TRAINED

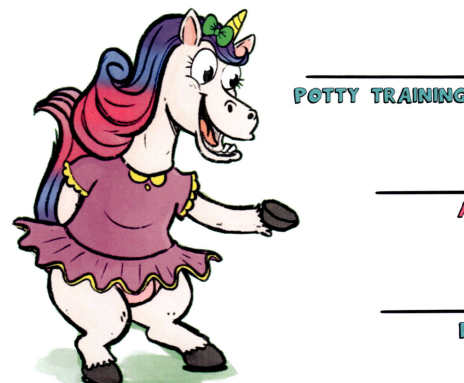

_____

POTTY TRAINING TRAINER / SURVIVOR

_____

AGE

_____

DATE

 Scan to view more fun Books!

WAIT!

If you enjoyed this book, consider leaving a review!

Scan here to review this book!

Made in the USA
Monee, IL
11 June 2022